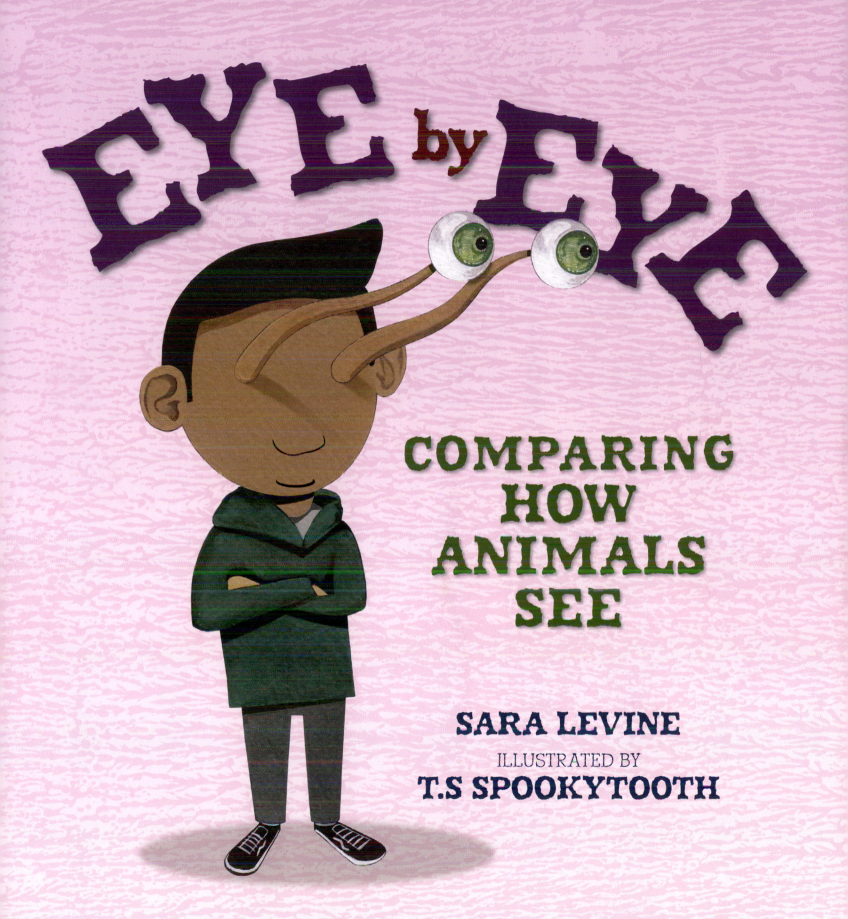

EYE by EYE

COMPARING HOW ANIMALS SEE

SARA LEVINE

ILLUSTRATED BY

T.S SPOOKYTOOTH

M Millbrook Press Minneapolis

For Ziah and Lija —S.L.

For Mom and Dad —T.S S.

Millbrook Press™
An imprint of Lerner Publishing Group, Inc.
241 First Avenue North
Minneapolis, MN 55401 USA

For reading levels and more information, look up this title at www.lernerbooks.com.

Designed by Danielle Carnito.
Main body text set in GFY Palmer Regular and King George Bold Clean Regular. Typefaces provided by Chank.
The illustrations in this book were created with acrylic paints and a little computer trickery.

Library of Congress Cataloging-in-Publication Data

Names: Levine, Sara (Veterinarian), author. | Spookytooth, T. S., illustrator.
Title: Eye by eye : comparing how animals see / Sara Levine ; illustrated by T.S. Spookytooth.
Description: Minneapolis : Millbrook Press, [2021] | Includes bibliographical references. | Audience: Ages 5–10 | Audience: Grades 2–3 | Summary: "This playful picture book will keep readers guessing as they find out how animal eyes are like- and unlike-those of starfish, owls, slugs, and more!"— Provided by publisher.
Identifiers: LCCN 2019049981 (print) | LCCN 2019049982 (ebook) | ISBN 9781541538382 (library binding) | ISBN 9781728401461 (ebook)
Subjects: LCSH: Eye—Juvenile literature.
Classification: LCC QL949 .L48 2021 (print) | LCC QL949 (ebook) | DDC 573.8/8—dc23

LC record available at https://lccn.loc.gov/2019049981
LC ebook record available at https://lccn.loc.gov/2019049982

Manufactured in the United States of America
1-45007-35838-2/7/2020

Have you ever wondered what it would be like to see the world through someone else's eyes?

What if those eyes belonged to an animal?

Most animals have eyes, but not all eyes are the same.

Some animals, for example, have more than two.

What kind of animal would you be if you had eight eyes?

A SPIDER!

This jumping spider has four big eyes on the front of its face. It also has four smaller eyes on the top of its head!

Most spiders have eight eyes, but some have as many as twelve.

What if you had six eyes, one located on the end of each of your six arms?

What kind of animal would you be, then?

A SEA STAR!

Different types of sea stars can have different numbers of arms, but each arm comes with its own eye. Their eyes don't work like human eyes do. Sea stars can see light, but they can't make out details.

Some animals have eyes that can move around a lot.

What kind of animal would you be if your eyes were at the ends of long stalks sticking out of the top of your head?

And when you felt like it, you could pull them back in toward yourself?

A SNAIL OR A SLUG!

These animals have eyes on the ends of their antennas. And they're retractable! Next time you find a snail or a slug, gently touch one of its eyes and watch the animal telescope it back into its head for protection.

What kind of animal would you be if you were born with an eye on each side of your head and, as you grew, one eye moved to a new place on your face?

A FLOUNDER!*

Flounders start their lives with one eye on each side of their heads like most fish. But then, over time, one eye travels so the grown-up flounder becomes a flat fish with its two eyes on top. This way, it can hide in the sand and still have both eyes peering up to keep a lookout.

The traveling eye takes three years to reach its adult location.

*Other fish, such as halibut, sole, and turbot, have eyes that do this too.

Other animals have eyes that can't move at all.

What kind of animal would you be if your eyeballs were completely stuck in place?

AN OWL!

Unlike humans, owls don't have sphere-shaped eyeballs. Their eyes are tube-shaped and are held in place by special bones.

Animal eyeballs don't always look like human eyeballs.

Some animals have pupils that are very different from our pupils. So what are pupils?

Pupils are the black circles in the middle of each of your eyes. They change size to let in the right amount of light so we can see well.

Most animals have round pupils like we do, but some animals have pupils in more unusual shapes.

What kind of animal would you be if your pupils were shaped like . . .

A rectangle?

Or an oval?

A GOAT!

Horses, deer, and sheep have rectangular pupils too. These animals also have eyes on the sides of their heads, instead of in front. These two things help animals see all around themselves so they know if a predator is coming.

A CAT!

Other animals with oval-shaped pupils are crocodiles, rattlesnakes, and foxes. These animals are all predators that hide and then ambush their prey. Oval-shaped pupils and eyes that face forward help a hunter to judge distance and plan its attack without making any movements that might scare away its meal.

What kind of animal would you be if your pupils were shaped like the letter W?

A CUTTLEFISH!

The W-shaped pupil is very unusual. Some scientists think it helps cuttlefish blend in with their surroundings. Others think it helps them see better underwater.

We think of eyeballs as being smooth, and most animals' eyeballs are. But some animals have eyes made up of many hexagon shapes, like you'd find on a soccer ball.

What kind of animal would you be if your eyes looked like that?

A FLY!*

Flies have compound eyes, which are made up of many hexagons. Each hexagon is like a separate eye, and they all work together to help the animal see.

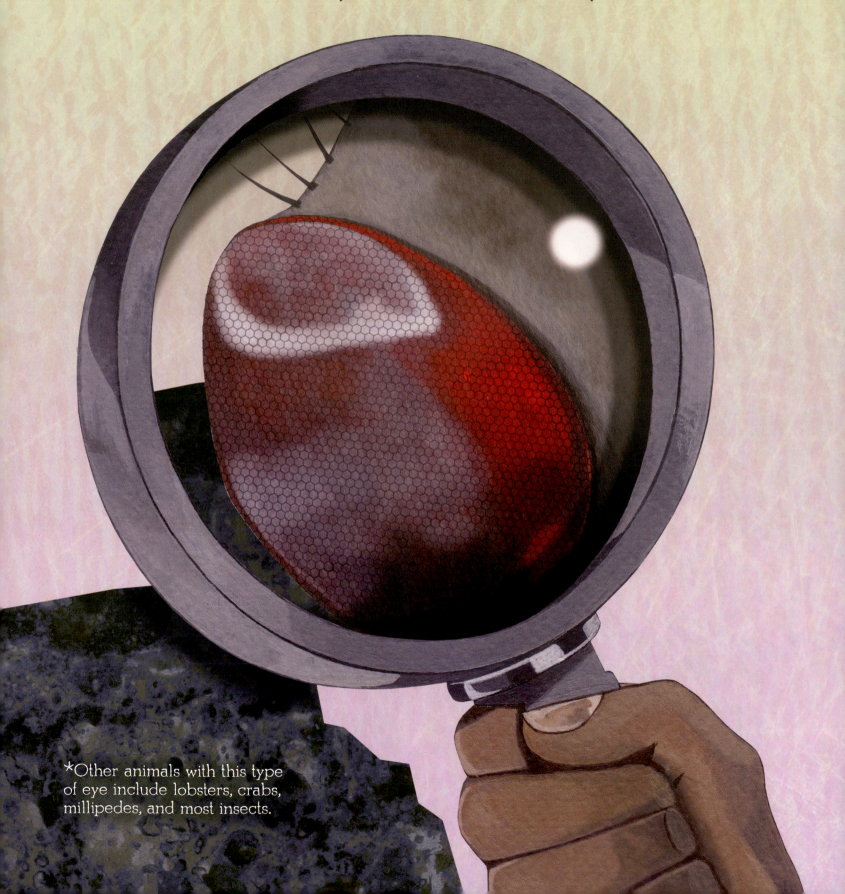

*Other animals with this type of eye include lobsters, crabs, millipedes, and most insects.

Some animals see colors differently than most humans do.

What kind of animal would you be if the colors green and red looked the same to you?

A DOG OR A CAT!
AND, SOMETIMES, EVEN A HUMAN!

Humans have three different types of cells in our eyes that help us see colors. These special cells are called cones. Cats and dogs have just two types of cones. Since they don't have the cone for seeing red and green, they can't see the difference between these colors.

Some people are born without this cone or have one that doesn't work, so they can't see red and green the way most people do either. A person who can't tell certain colors apart is said to be color-blind.

This page shows how a cat or a dog would see the image on the facing page.

Some animals have more cones in their eyes than humans have. Butterflies and birds have four different types of cones.

What would the world look like if you were a butterfly or a bird?

SORRY, WE HAVE NO IDEA, BUT WE CAN GUESS IT'S QUITE COLORFUL!

We have to use our imaginations, since our eyes can't give us this information. But it's pretty cool to know that there are things that exist out there that humans can't see at all.

Here's a last one for you:
What kind of animal
would you be if your
eyes could read the
letters in this WORD?

A HUMAN!

Did you get that one?
If so, you are a human who is using your eyes to read.

Other animals also use their eyes to read signs. A bee can read lines on a flower petal so it knows where to land when it needs a drink of nectar. And a dog can read the body language of another dog. It knows that the bared teeth and raised hackles mean STAY AWAY.

So far, we haven't discovered another animal that uses its eyes to read human writing in a book.

BUT WE WILL KEEP LOOKING, OF COURSE.

WANT TO LEARN MORE ABOUT WHAT IT'S LIKE TO SEE THROUGH THE EYES OF AN ANIMAL? TRY THESE ACTIVITIES!

How much do sea stars see? Tie a winter scarf around your head as a blindfold. If you keep your eyes open, you can see light coming from some places and maybe the outline of a few things, right? Well, that's about as much as a sea star can see.

How do owls see the world? Hold your head completely still, and try looking to your right. And now, look to your left. Look up to the ceiling. Look down to the floor. *You* can do this because you can move your eyes.

But if you had owl eyes, you couldn't. Make your fists into the shape of a pair of binoculars, and hold them up to your eyes to peer through. Now try looking side to side and up and down without moving your head. You can't see much, can you? This is how it is having owl eyeballs that can't move. You are stuck seeing only what is in front of you. You have to turn your head to see. Fortunately for owls, they are able to turn their heads almost all the way around to see what's going on to the sides. To see above and below, owls bob their heads up and down. Peering through your fist-shaped binoculars, try moving your head around like an owl to see how owls view the world.

A CLOSE-UP LOOK AT PUPILS

A pupil is the dark circle at the center of each of your eyes. It's actually a hole that lets light into your eyeball. When it's dark out, your pupils get larger, or dilate, to let more light in. And, when it's bright out, your pupils get smaller, or constrict, to block out some of the light. Grab a mirror to have a look. Try turning a light on and off while looking in your mirror, and watch how your pupils change size.

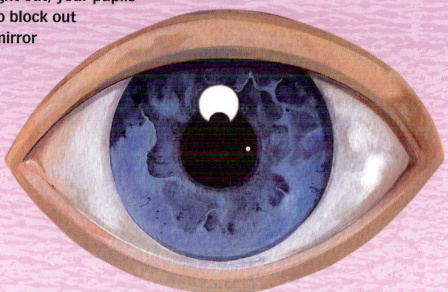

GLOSSARY

color-blind: not able to tell the difference between certain colors

compound: made up of two or more parts

cone: a cell inside the eye that detects color and bright light

hackles: hairs that stand up on the neck and back of a dog or another animal when it is angry, excited, or scared

hexagon: a flat shape with six straight sides and six angles

nectar: sweet liquid food that plants make for pollinators to eat

predator: an animal that hunts and eats other animals

prey: an animal hunted by other animals for food

pupil: the dark opening in the center of the eye that lets light in

retractable: able to be pulled back or in

FURTHER READING

Books

Duprat, Guillaume. *Eye Spy: Wild Ways Animals See the World*. Tonbridge, Kent, UK: What on Earth Books, 2018.

Holland, Mary. *Animal Eyes*. Mt. Pleasant, SC: Arbordale, 2015.

Jenkins, Steve. *Eye to Eye: How Animals See the World*. Boston: Houghton Mifflin Harcourt, 2014.

Markle, Sandra. *What If You Had Animal Eyes?* New York: Scholastic, 2017.

Winston, Robert. *My Amazing Body Machine*. New York: DK, 2017.

Websites

Your Amazing Eyes!
https://www.natgeokids.com/nz/discover/science/general-science/human-eye/
Find out five facts about your eyes and how they work.

Your Eyes
https://kidshealth.org/en/kids/eyes.html
Check out a diagram showing all the parts of your eye along with detailed explanations of how those parts work together to help you see. Also learn ways to keep your eyes healthy and safe.